THE PERF|
VETERINARY CONSULT

CONSULTING TECHNIQUES AND
BEHAVIOURS IN SMALL ANIMAL PRACTICE

Dr Sanjay Mangabhai

Contents

Part 1: CONSULTING TECHNIQUES

Introduction

Veterinary Medicine is both an art and a science. Most of what is covered here is about the art. Much of the emphasis in formal veterinary education still focuses heavily on diagnostic skills, even though we know that consultation skills, including the ability to convey trust, competence and confidence, also result in better care of patients and additionally improved job satisfaction. As veterinary professionals **we are born to make a difference**, and how we do this depends a great deal on our performance in the consulting room.

These guidelines are taken from my online operations manual of the practices I owned and managed for almost 20 years. Practices can often be very personal places which is reflected in things like dress code, length of appointments, medical protocols, exam reports, and whether nurses assist the doctors in consulting rooms. These guidelines, therefore, are not intended to be all-encompassing but are designed to reflect what worked well and was successful for my practice and will hopefully work well for you.

A lot of what is covered in here seems obvious and something that you would already know.   However, whilst that may be true, it is unfortunately not common practice. **Knowing it** and **doing it** are two different things. Just like surgical skills, it takes time and committed practice to develop competency in these techniques and embed them into your habits. Consulting skills can, and should, be practised and developed throughout one's career and not only when you are just starting out. My hope is that these guidelines will be invaluable to recent graduates and a useful reminder to the more experienced.

Because very few of us *see* other vets and nurses actually consulting in real time and real situations, most of what we do is by assumption and deduction from various sources. Role play, "sitting in" on consults, and watching videos with actors is valuable but is still rather artificial and contrived. We had CCTV in our consulting rooms for many years and found that they give us an invaluable insight into what worked and what did not in real situations.

Also, unless you have a method of standardizing and appraising consulting techniques (such as an examination form/report and client surveys), then it is very difficult to get any kind of consistency and predictability regarding the consult process, and therefore, of the experience for the client, especially between different veterinary surgeons and practices.

Understanding a Consultation

The consultation is the **HEART** of veterinary practice. The majority of work generated in a veterinary practice starts in the consulting room. This makes **the consulting room the most important room in the practice!** How "busy" a practice's consultations are determines how busy the entire practice is in general, and consultations have a direct link to total practice revenues.

However accomplished your surgical, diagnostic and other **technical** skills are, you will not get the chance to use them if your **soft** or **communication** skills fail to persuade clients to let you. We know that consultation skills, including the ability to convey **trust**, **competence**, and **confidence** also result in better care of patients, increased client satisfaction and additionally improves personal job satisfaction.

A consultation in first opinion small animal veterinary practice may be defined as reviewing a patient's medical history, performing a physical examination, making recommendations for further investigations, treatment and care, and performing minor consulting room procedures.

Success in the consulting room depends on much more than clinical knowledge, diagnosis, and treatment. The **quality of care** that clients opt for (and that pets then receive), **your career success** and the **success of the practice** itself, is highly dependent on having a successful consultation experience.

Consulting technique (of which communication is an essential part) is thus very important to the success of **any** veterinary surgeon and **any** veterinary practice.

As a veterinary surgeon, unless you have a clear understanding of what a consultation is, and how to achieve a successful consultation, you will fail your patients and your clients. Developing good consultation skills takes **time** *and* **practice**. It involves self-criticism and self-awareness. Consultation skills can and should be developed **throughout one's career**.

Objectives of Consultation Techniques

1. To ensure that the consultation/examination is **repeatedly** and **predictably**:

   - ✓ Consistent
   - ✓ Comprehensive
   - ✓ Efficient
   - ✓ Client friendly

2. To help build rapport and trusting relationships with clients (client bonding) by ensuring **effective, concise, empathetic,** and **understandable communication**.

3. To ensure the right information is gathered and that a good treatment and/or management plan is devised

4. To ensure the **maximum value** of the consultation process for the pet, the client, and the practice

Look Professional

Appearing professional (you and the practice in general) sets you up for success before you actually say or do anything medical. It puts you in good stead, sets the right tone, gives confidence to the client that they are in good hands, so to speak.

Present Yourself as a Medical Professional

- ✓ Dress: coats, tunics and trousers should be clean, wrinkle-free, and not soiled by pet fur, blood and other stains. Shoes must be neat, clean, with no scuffs and polished as appropriate.
- ✓ Hair should neat and well-groomed
- ✓ Shirts, polo tops and blouses should buttoned
- ✓ Name badges are all worn just below top left corner of the shoulder
- ✓ A stethoscope should be *visible*, either draped around the neck or placed neatly in a coat pocket
- ✓ Visibly wash and dry hands in the consulting room between patients so that is obvious to the client
- ✓ Be organised and have all needed instruments ready for use: otoscope, ophthalmoscope, thermometer, clippers, etc - organisation makes the consultation more efficient

Scrub (theatre) tops are **not** advisable in the consulting room or reception area.

Studies show that when a doctor **looks professional**, then clients are more likely to:

- Trust them
- Believe they are competent
- View them as meticulous and serious
- Share private information more readily with them

Wearing a white lab coat/tunic, name badge and stethoscope gives a doctor **credibility**.

Do not appear **hurried** and **disorganised**. Do not leave the room if at all possible – this will not be necessary if you *are* organised.

Try to present a **calm** and **in-control** attitude (equanimity) to every client even **if** things may be stressful otherwise. There is no need to show your stress, dissatisfaction, annoyance, tiredness, etc. to them.

BE ON TIME. Running late **is** one of the pitfalls of veterinary medicine and one of the top things that frustrate clients – and receptionists, who then have to manage client expectations and mitigate their irritations.

Prepare the Consulting Room

Ensure the consulting room is **clean, tidy** and **pleasant smelling** for each and every consultation. This sets you and the client up for a good and efficient consult.

- **Tidy** any used equipment away e.g. clippers, ophthalmoscope, auriscope heads, etc
- Ensure the consulting table is **cleaned** and **freshly disinfected** after each patient. Spray the consulting able with a suitable disinfectant e.g. Anigene® and wipe clean with paper towel.
- Ensure the floor is clean - no fur, secretions, blood stains, etc
- Ensure a **pleasant smell**. Use odour sprays as necessary to neutralize any unpleasant odours. (It is a good idea to spray a pet's "back end" with a safe and suitable odour spray after expressing anal glands).
- Have a dustpan and hand-held vacuum in the consulting rooms. Use the hoover (or dustpan and brush) to remove fur and other dry, hard materials e.g. clipped nails

Know the Reason for the Appointment

Check the appointment diary ***in advance*** for the reason for the visit, e.g.

- Puppy/kitten vaccination
- Booster vaccination
- Illness symptoms (e.g. vomiting, not eating, lame, coughing, wound, etc)
- Post-op assessment
- Clip nails
- Anal gland expression
- Euthanasia
- Etc.

Knowing the reason for the appointment helps you:

- ✓ **Prepare mentally** for the appointment (your attitude and approach to a puppy vaccination is very different to how you would approach a euthanasia appointment)

- ✓ **Re-assures the client** that you are expecting them and are familiar with their problem or the service required

- ✓ Allows you to **prepare and organise** the consulting room for the anticipated procedure (e.g. ensure clippers are clean)

Check the Client Details and Previous Patient History

Familiarise yourself with the client and patient history. Look for information in the medical history that you may need to consider and might influence your decisions, e.g. reactions to certain drugs.

Please do this *BEFORE* calling them into the consulting room. This also prevents needing to constantly refer to the computer which can be both distracting and disengaging for both you and the client.

- ✓ Know the **names** of the **client** AND the **pet**
- ✓ Go into the patient's record to look at **previous visit histories**
- ✓ If a new reason, then look for any **specific notes** regarding:
  - ▪ Possible drug reactions
  - ▪ Allergies
  - ▪ Temperament issues (aggressive pets need more care)
  - ▪ Etc.
- ✓ Ensure the client has no disabilities which need special attention e.g. poor hearing

Invite the Client and Pet into the Examination Room

FIRST IMPRESSIONS MATTER! If a client perceives you as being stressed, tired, rushed, disorganised, unhappy, etc., it sets the consultation off on the wrong footing! **Clients don't need to know if you're having a bad day!**

From the waiting room, invite the client (e.g. with pet name "Sammy" and owner's surname "King") into the cons room saying:

"Sammy King, please."

Please use the client's and the pet's name. Unless you are absolutely certain, **avoid** using Mrs, Miss and Ms as you can often get these wrong. Only use the client's first name if invited to do so. Then make a note of the first name in the client record, so that you do not forget it. Client data on most practice management systems only includes the surname.

If a nurse has called the client into the consulting room then come from behind the consulting table and **welcome** returning clients back and **introduce yourself** to new clients or those you have not seen before. Shake hands with the client. E.g.

"Hello Mr Robinson! Nice to see you again" or

Introduce yourself, "Hello Mr Robinson. I'm Tracey, it's good to meet you".

You may shake their hands. Next greet their children. Then **greet the pet by name.** Give the pet a **cuddle, hug, pat, stroke** - depending on temperament and size; in other words, **touch the pet!**
Use the client's name and the pet's name frequently. Use the clients name at least 3 times during the consultation. Ask clients to use your first name – this creates a friendly atmosphere.

Call the clients into the consulting room according to appointment and arrival times. Some clients come in early for appointments; either see them first or ask the receptionist to explain that you are seeing a client who had an earlier appointment before seeing them. Please don't simply ignore them.

Tell clients exactly what is going to happen during the consultation; this is called **signposting**. This helps alleviate any possible anxiety they may feel about the experience and what may or may not happen. You can say,

"To start with I'm going to ask you a few questions about Smokey and what has been going on. Then I'll perform a thorough physical examination. After this we'll talk about how to sort the problem out. Is that alright?"

Observe the client - you can tell a lot from facial expressions (interest, disinterest, happy, frustrated, worried, etc). this allows you to personalise your communication to the client e.g. matching and mirroring.

Try to **face the client** at all times and **not** turn your back towards them. Write your notes after they have left the room, especially if using the computer means you have to face your back to them. It can be difficult to avoid letting the computer become the focus, especially if there is potentially useful information that you may want to refer to. Practice getting the information you might need beforehand.

Please get the SEX of the patient right! Clients seem to really dislike it when you get this wrong and they take great satisfaction in pointing out your error! Many pet names don't give us any clue about the gender. Please **do not guess** as you will invariably get it wrong. So, check the patient record and *make sure* that you know.

Take the Patient History

Getting a good patient history is about defining the problem. If you don't correctly identify the problem, how will you find the right solution?

You can only make the best medical decisions if you have the **right information**. <u>Do not</u> make impulsive assumptions about why a client has brought their pet in.

Obtaining a good clinical history is often a very important part of reaching the right diagnosis or making the right decision about the next step to take. **The better the clinical history you get, the better *and* quicker your decisions will be**. So don't skip it or rush it.

Confirm to the client the reason for the visit: e.g.

"Mr Andrews, you've brought Max here today for his booster vaccination. Is that correct?"

"Mrs Smith, you've brought Smokey here today because he has not eaten for 2 days? Is that correct?"

If there is no clear reason for the visit, simply ask,

"How may I help you today?" Try to determine what the clients hopes to get out of the consultation today.

If the appointment is a progress medical evaluation (a repeat visit) then you need to enquire about the progress:

"How do you think Toffee is doing? Is she any better, much the same, or worse?"

"How are you managing with the medication (wound cleaning, restricted exercise, etc)?"

Listen Carefully (Active Listening)

Appear attentive and maintain eye contact as much as possible - without staring. Good **listening** underpins effective history taking. A good history can often reveal the likely diagnosis in many illnesses and also lead to the diagnosis *faster*. People are more satisfied with their consulting room experience when they **FEEL** that the doctor was actually listening to them. It is generally **not** acceptable to make detailed notes *as* the client speaks. If you must, jot down single words to jog your memory later.

Repeat back to the client the concern/s they have raised to show that you *understand* the problems. **Paraphrase** (i.e. using similar, but not the same, words and phrases) rather than use exactly the same words (as it could annoy some clients). This is a particularly useful way to clarify that *your understanding of the problem is the **same** as the client's*. This is also called "replay and confirm". It sounds simple enough, but it does take quite a bit of **practice** to become good at it.

Remember to **be silent** (stop talking and DON'T INTERRUPT clients) after asking a question. Only interrupt for clarification (e.g. "Was that before or after eating? Was that once or more than once?") and if the client is talking for more than a minute or so without adding anything useful. Most responses don't go on for more than a minute. Not interrupting also avoids receiving complaints that "The vet/nurse did not listen to me".

Ask questions that are **OPEN**, giving the client the opportunity to expand. Closed questions demand limited answers ("Yes" or "No") or are often **leading** (i.e. encourages the client to tell you what they think you want to know).

"How is Smokey's appetite?" open question

"Is Smokey eating?" closed question

When necessary, encourage the client to give more information by saying "Please continue" or "Go on" and/or **nodding.**

Before moving onto the next step remember to ask, "Is there anything else that I can help you with today?"

It can be tempting to move quickly to a physical examination and investigation or treatment once you feel that you have a provisional diagnosis. **Avoid** this, and make sure you have gathered **all** the patient and symptom data that you can.

People love dealing with professionals that listen, who hear, see and feel things the way they do!

There are generally 3 types of client:

1. **Auditory** person: they tend to be this type if they never stop talking.
    Need to use phrases like: How does that <u>sound</u> to you? That <u>sounds</u> good to me, etc

2. **Visual** person: they tend to watch everything you do.
    Need to use phrases like: Can you <u>see</u>? I <u>see</u> exactly what you mean, etc.

3. **Kinaesthetic** person: they usually don't say much but feel things. They use phrases like: I didn't feel like he needed that. I felt differently about that.
    Need to use phrases like: I can understand how you <u>feel</u>.

History taking is a skill that requires practice and continual refinement.

Perform a Comprehensive Physical Examination

The Physical Examination is the **CORNERSTONE of veterinary medicine.**

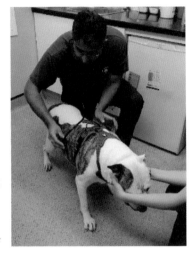

Despite advancements in technology, the physical examination and patient history remain **core medical skills** and form the foundation of arriving at a presumptive or differential diagnosis and determining the investigative and treatment steps needed.

More mistakes are made by **not asking** and **not looking**, than by not knowing.

You can make the **best decisions _only_** if you have the **right information**. Getting accurate information from a physical examination by performing it accurately and thoroughly every time will lead to drawing the right conclusions. Together with a good clinical history it will allow you to make the **best medical decisions** about diagnoses or next investigative steps. All your actions and decisions will flow from accurately defining or characterising what the actual problem is.

Develop the habit of following the same steps of the examination in the same order - this creates consistency and minimises the risk of overlooking something. Perform a _comprehensive_ physical examination in a _systematic_ (i.e. methodical) manner:

nose-to-tail for **dogs** and tail-to-nose for cats.

The goal is to ensure a thorough, consistent, and systematic physical examination is performed **every single time**. A poor physical examination often results in oversights (i.e. missing things), inaccurate diagnoses, unnecessary tests and other investigations, and ultimately in poor patient care and outcomes, and usually increased costs.

As a rule, a physical examination is made up of **both** GENERAL OBSERVATION and HANDS-ON EXAMINATION (palpation, percussion, auscultation). Remember that the VISUAL IMPRESSION of the patient is a *powerful* impression and should not be overlooked. Spend a few moments simply observing the pet. What is its demeanour? Does it look healthy or not? Is posture and mobility normal? If you have presence of mind and are observant you can gain a lot of information *before you have even touched* the patient.

A **comprehensive** physical examination consists of a **12 Body System Examination**. Many pets are good at masking their illness from us; so only an experienced veterinary surgeon can perform an accurate examination to determine a pet's state of illness *or wellness*.

Sometimes clients may wonder why you are examining the entire body when they brought their pet in for a specific problem e.g. sore eye. This is what to say to the client:

"So that we don't overlook anything, we like to perform a complete physical examination of every pet we see".

Focus on the problem area *AFTER* performing a complete physical examination.

The act of examining or treating should be made **very obvious** to the client. Don't do anything "secretively". Use the thermometer, stethoscope, otoscope, ophthalmoscope, etc. as appropriate.

A *comprehensive* **physical examination** is performed for:

- All initial illness consultations
- Primary vaccinations
- Booster vaccinations
- 6-month health assessments
- Pre-anaesthetic examinations
- Prescription health evaluations
- Progress evaluations where a clinical diagnosis remains undetermined

And an **examination report** is completed (see Comprehensive Physical Exam, CPE, form mentioned below)

All patients must be weighed each time that they are examined, even if they came in a few days ago.

Temperature, Pulse and Respiration measurements should be taken whenever practical.

A **dental grade/stage** is given (*and discussed*) for *every* patient - unless unable to examine the mouth e.g. aggressive patients. Make a note on the CPE form or clinical record why this was not done. Please familiarise yourself with how to perform dental staging.

A **Body Condition Score** is given (*and discussed*) for *every* patient. Please familiarise yourself with the Body Condition Scoring system.

Please make any **notes** on the CPE form in a prominent colour e.g. **RED** or **BLUE** colour. This makes it more visual, so drawing attention to it.

A FOLLOW-UP RECOMMENDATION IS MADE AFTER *EVERY* CONSULTATION, even if it is for a vaccination in 1 years' time (**Forward Appointment Booking** system).

Where a pet is doing well - then make an appropriate note on the form to highlight this. E.g. **"wonderful teeth," "really healthy coat," "very cute puppy," "extremely well behaved"** etc.
A copy of the CPE form **must** be **emailed** (or given**)** to the client.

Whenever a body system was **_not_** examined for whatever reason, then **please say so** in the appropriate section of the CPE form. We do not want to mislead clients in any way.

We recommend a comprehensive (12 body system) physical examination **twice** a year on all "**normal**" pets. Because **pets age faster than humans**, having a physical examination every six months for a pet is like a human having an examination every few years. Pets cannot talk to communicate how they feel so often they are on a faster path toward illness than humans.

For a 15-20minute appointment, we have 10-15 minutes of actual "vet-client **face-time**" (this is the time the vet is **actually facing** and **talking** to the client: 10 mins in a 15-min consult and 15 mins in a 20-min consult). Please give the client and patient 10/15 minutes of your undivided attention. Clients generally have an **expectation** for **something to be done** to their pet: wound cleaned, ears checked, temperature taken, injection given, etc.

To give yourself adequate time to **examine patients thoroughly** and **explain things fully**, it is expected that you **use your very capable nurses to perform all the tasks that they can do** (and are permitted to do by the relevant governing body) e.g. recording patient histories and some clinical findings, pricing up, preparing estimates, preparing handouts, clearing the cons room after, etc. (This mainly applies to practices where nurses are routinely present in the consulting room)

Use the Comprehensive Physical Examination (CPE) **form** and fill it out completely. It is completed for all initial illness and primary booster vaccination appointments. The CPE form forms part of the medical record. Where one is not available then the SAME information needs to be recorded in the patient record. If a nurse is available then she will perform the TPR, give a dental grade and BCS (body condition score) and fill out the relevant sections of the form; otherwise you will have to do this. Ensure that a copy of the CPE form is emailed to the client.

Be gentle with the pet and talk to and involve any children who are present.

If a procedure could potentially hurt or *look like it could* (e.g. restraining a cat), then *forewarn* the client. E.g.

"Mr Bradshaw sometimes this injection stings and Smokey may cry out"

If the pet is fractious then ask the client's permission to take the pet to the prep room where it is more inclined to be less confident – this presents a better professional image. Be sure that the owner approves though!

"Mr Smith, it will be better do this in the prep room where it may be easier to hold Smokey and …… take the blood sample …. clip the wound …. place an intravenous catheter …. etc."

Use this opportunity to have the client read relevant information or watch a video, etc.

Talk in a quiet tone that not only soothes the pet but keeps the client informed of what you are doing. Look, feel, smell, listen, and as you do so **tell the client** <u>what you are doing</u> and <u>what you are finding</u>.

Using An Examination Form

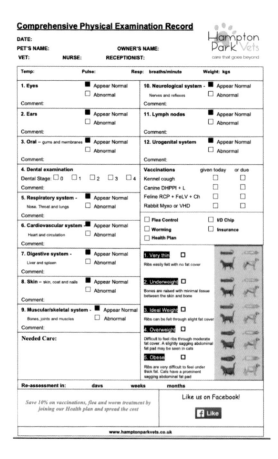

Having to complete this form ensures that a thorough, consistent and systematic physical examination is performed every single time.

The completed form is emailed to clients and confirms to them:

✓ what was checked

✓ what needs to be done and

✓ when to come back for a re-visit

Verbalising The Physical Examination

Talk to the client during the exam, **verbalising** your findings and observations, both normal *and* abnormal; this **adds** **value** to the consultation/ examination by explaining (and making it obvious) to the client what you are doing and finding e.g.

"Smokey's eyes appear fine, he has evidence of dental disease (show the client), his coat seems healthy though I can see some flea dirt, his heart sounds fine, lungs have clear breath sounds, etc."

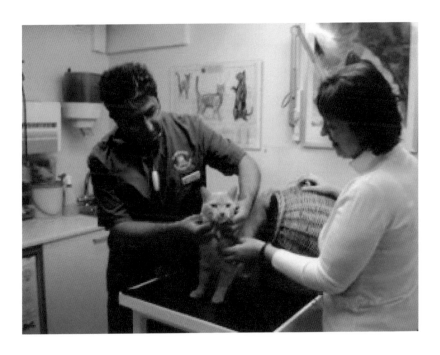

During any physical examination of a patient, vets should discuss what they're seeing, hearing, smelling, and touching. Clients want to know they were right to spend the money and time to take their pet to your practice. They want to see that the physical examination matters. Find something about which to genuinely compliments the pet - owners like really appreciate this.

Talk to and involve any children who are present.

Keeping a **running commentary** reassures the client of what you are doing, keeps them engaged and later helps with explaining any abnormalities you may have found - all of which helps tremendously with the perception of value.

It is up to you to explain each observation made to the client. People want to hear that you are doing a good job with their pet. The most important part of the vaccination process is the physical examination. Most findings/observations tend to be normal. Tell clients this, they love to hear that their pets are normal and healthy.

Explain what you are thinking and doing every step of the way. Your voice can soothe both the patient and the client.

The nurse in the consulting room needs to understand everything that you have said and be able to explain it to clients afterwards. This is a good test of the effectiveness of your explanations.

Discuss Examination Findings - Clearly and Fully Explain

Veterinary medicine's biggest challenge is explaining exactly **what** we do for pets and **why**! It is difficult to be an effective veterinary practitioner unless you learn how to explain effectively.

We are **educators** on pet healthcare and most of the client education that we do happens in the consulting room.

We need to **EDUCATE** clients in the consulting room with the same passion we spend treating and preventing disease in pets.

Selling is what we end up doing when we give **poor explanations** for needed care. And we NEVER want to sell anything in veterinary medicine - and frankly, most of us don't particularly want to _sell_ anything, anyway.

So again, **EXPLAIN**, don't **sell**!
Educate, don't pressurize.

Learning how to explain medical concepts is fundamental to enabling clients to **understand** clinical findings and what the next steps are. It's a bit like learning to give clear and accurate directions to a certain address that they have never been to before (without using a SATNAV). It can be argued that without learning to explain well, your clients easily get "lost" i.e. confused and frustrated, leading to poor compliance with recommendations and hence poorer medical outcomes.

Try not to rely only on verbal explanations. Use all the different forms of communication at your disposal:

a. **Give educational handouts** - these are either in-house handouts or pharmaceutical company leaflets. These help to reinforce recommendations. It helps if these have good pictures and diagrams, rather than just written material.

b. **Draw diagrams and write short explanatory notes**. A **white board** in the consulting room is a great tool - use it to explain or demonstrate. Don't worry if you have poor artistic talent. The time spent drawing and writing down important points also allows you to clarify your thoughts. You can also use **plain A4 paper** to write and draw things on; and which the client can then take home to help jog their memories, and also explain findings and recommendations to family members.

c. **Use models and visual aids**. These are usually anatomical models and posters (ears, eyes, joints, skin, etc)

d. **Show short videos**. Most computers/tablets in consulting rooms have internet access. Become familiar with good videos that you can easily and repeatably use.

a. **Give links to relevant websites**. I find veterinarypartner.com especially useful

When you do this, you can overcome most misunderstandings.

Why is this all important? Because **clients typically remember 7-10% of what was said in a consultation** and, just like us, they need tools to *help them remember*.

Use Simple Language

Use **language** that the client **understands**.

Using language and medical terms that a **12-year old** can understand is generally what to aim for. The aim is to try to explain things at the client's level of *medical* understanding. Many clients give the *impression* that they understand to avoid seeming foolish in front of *you*, the professional. It is better to OVER-COMMUNICATE when sharing new ideas or difficult concepts. Studies show that people do not absorb as much information as we think they did.

Professionals generally tend to suffer from a type of cognitive bias where they find it difficult to know or remember what it feels like **not** to know something that they already know very well, and usually take for granted. So we **assume** clients know what we are talking about when we explain things, as it seems so obvious to us. Try not to make assumptions; you can often evaluate whether a client understands what you are explaining by paying attention carefully to what they say - the type of language they use and also the type of questions they might ask.

Although it can be a little daunting when faced with clients who have a medical background it is still **wise not to assume** that they can fully understand veterinary medical terms. Human medical jargon may not always translate into that of veterinary, and human medicine also tends to be quite specific/specialised. It is, however, worth being mindful of their

knowledge and let *them* inform you that they understand what you are explaining. You may say something like "Please let me know if I'm explaining this too simply".

Repeat important points and check to see if the client understands. (Ask "Have I explained this OK?" or "Do you think you will be able to explain this to you wife/husband/children, etc.?)

Show What You Find

Show the client what you have found in your examination.
Show them the bad teeth and inflamed gums, the waxy ears, corneal ulcer, etc.

Show them pictures, diagrams, models, drawings, videos, bladder stones, preserved parasites.

Don't worry too much about offending clients with gross samples or pictures, etc. - they are the reality and will serve to motivate them to prevent these parasites and medical problems.

Remember to take the time to thoroughly explain your **normal** _and_ **abnormal** findings. Go through **all** the abnormal findings starting with the most urgent.

Chunking - Give Morsels of Information

It is important **HOW** potentially complex information is communicated. It helps with understanding and memory if not too much information is given at one time, especially about something unfamiliar or complex.

Chunking, in simple terms, is a process whereby information is broken down into smaller pieces, so helping to understand it, and remember it. As a guide, try to give 1 to 3 sentence chunks of medical information at a time. Then keep quiet to allow for questions and/or ask, "Do you have any questions so far?"

Discuss Next Steps - Investigations and Tests

Today, quality medicine makes it necessary to **involve the client**, and work with them in a **spirit of cooperation**; not simply tell them what needs to be done, as in days gone by. This undoubtedly leads to the client having a better understanding of what the problem is, so that **shared decision making** in the best next steps can be taken.

Also, remember that clients are increasingly more informed and knowledgeable about healthcare in general, and pet healthcare in particular, because of easy access to information especially online and through social media. This can be positive in that it will usually make it easier for them to understand medical concepts and also help them ask better questions to clarify things.

Explain to clients what the next steps are to resolve the problem.
Include your diagnosis (or differential diagnoses), likely outcome (prognosis) and cost. You must provide clients with adequate information making sure that they are aware of

- **what will be done** with their pet
- **what the risks are**
- **what the prognosis is,** and
- **what alternatives** might be available

Be **specific** about what is **needed!**

Using "**we**" instead of "**I**" makes it feel like a **team effort**. Say things like,

"This is what _we_ need to do to alleviate the pain"

instead of,

"This is what _I_ need to do to alleviate the pain".

Obtain consent. Record it in the medical notes e.g.

"Discussed blood test and urinalysis and Mr Smith consented to go ahead".

Be prepared to give more information to further explain reasons for the recommendations.

Set a specific date for the procedure/test/progress evaluation/etc. **at the time** of the consultation.

Make Recommendations

Always recommend <u>ONLY</u> what the pet genuinely **NEEDS**! How well a vet *explains the reasons for a recommendation* is what drives **compliance** and the perception of **value**! Remember that we need to **educate to motivate** clients to take our recommendations.

In other words, give the client evidence for the needed care. Begin with the end in mind i.e. what is the desired outcome (healed wound, easily jump into car, stop scratching, less stiff, pain free, eat more/less, etc.) then take steps to achieve it.

Give clients the treatment recommendations and expectations **upfront** (i.e. tell them all that is going to be needed, or is going to happen, now *and* in the future) e.g.

- New puppy:
  "We're going to change the diet 3 times - puppy food, adult food, senior diet"
  "I know that you're going to be tempted with cheaper brands when this free sample runs out"

- Warn of potential ***breed specific*** problems:
  - ✓ ear problems in Spaniels and Labs
  - ✓ joint problems in Labs
  - ✓ heart disease in CKCS
  - ✓ brachiocephalic syndrome in bulldogs and pugs

- Warn of Senior diseases
  - ✓ Renal disease
  - ✓ Arthritis
  - ✓ Hearing and vision deterioration

If **forewarned**, then they are **not totally surprised** when the problems do happen. Also, they can take steps to **prevent problems** from occurring or **catch them early**.

Until you <u>believe</u> in yourself, clients will <u>never</u> believe in you!

Pet owners are 7 times more likely to accept a vet's recommendations if the language used is clear and unambiguous (Veterinary Team Brief)

Talk about the *Benefits* and Give Clients the *Best Options* <u>first</u>

Explain the <u>*benefits*</u> of treatments, products and drugs. Always **emphasise** the benefits of treatments, procedures or products before you list the down sides, but ***never, ever fail*** to tell clients about the potential problems.

Benefits like how the pet might feel/behave:
- Pain free
- More active
- Pleasant breath
- Eat better
- Scratch less
- Climb stairs easier, etc

Benefits that affect the owner:

- Better behaved pet
- Less smelly breath, coat
- Undisturbed sleep because pet is more comfortable
- Not have to lift arthritic pets into /out of car, etc.

Answer the "***What's in it for me?***" question that clients think about but don't necessarily ask. There has to be something in it for the client, i.e. a frustration/worry/concern that needs to be satisfied e.g.

"We want to perform a pre-anaesthetic blood test *because* it's important to make sure Smokey is healthy enough to undergo anaesthesia."

If possible, **sit down** and explain the issues with clients. Studies with human doctors show that clients perceive that they got better care if the doctor **sat down** with them, no matter how briefly.

Discuss Treatment Options

Present the **best** treatment options **first** then, keep quiet and allow the client to say "yes" or ask further questions.

Let the client decide (not you) if the treatment is too expensive.

Your recommendations can easily cost a client several hundred pounds in an instant. Consider breaking treatment up over time or giving more than one treatment option. If you do offer alternative treatment options, don't undercut your best or preferred plan.

Example of a good approach:

"Our best treatment plan is Plan Number 1. This is preferred because …. Another course of action is Plan Number 2. However, here there is a greater chance of these worrying issues ……. or we need to be more careful of ……. "

An example of a not-so-good approach:

"The best course of action is Plan Number 1, because …. We could try Plan Number 2, where we … We could also think about Plan Number 3 ……. "

Explain **honestly,** openly and **clearly** the risks involved with less-than-ideal or cheaper options. But remember that clients may NEED to choose less-than-ideal treatments for good reason e.g. affordability.

Do not **trivialise** a client's concerns, point of view, or questions. *It is really not necessary to humiliate or embarrass clients for what may be for them a difficult **financial** or **lifestyle** decision.* **Be empathetic** - this allows you to see the situation from the client's perspective and not draw negative conclusions. "I respect your decision" is sometimes all you need to say.

Involve the Client

It is important to try to involve the client in the **treatment decision-making process** and the **management plan**. The best medical care is often achieved as a **partnership** between the client and the vet or practice. Ultimately, the client has the choice of whether to accept your medical management plan or not.

Compliance is also much more likely if the client has been made to feel part of the decisions made e.g. ask:

"Is this something you think you can do at home?"
"Is there anything else we can do that you think might help?"
"How do you think we can keep the Elizabethan collar on all the time?"

Involving clients helps to **engage** them in their pet's medical care which then makes them more likely to accept your recommendations, follow through with treatments, and also take a more active role in managing the care. You can prescribe a treatment that you know will work, but if the client does not carry out the treatment as prescribed, then it's not going to "fix" the problem. You often have to develop and use skills of **education**, **demonstration** and **motivation**.

Agreement to a medical management plan can often be a **negotiation** between the vet and the client, and the best negotiations are ones where *everyone benefits*.

Involve several people in the treatment or management plan. The more people (team and family members) who are involved, and the more **support** they are getting, the *more likely* they are to follow your instructions. Encourage team members to ask clients how they are getting on with giving tablets, confining their pet, etc. and advise them to *offer support and guidance* where needed.

Consider the Clients Abilities

You may have to consider the client's **lifestyle** when discussing treatment options. How will they manage with giving medication every 4 to 6 hours, or more frequently, if they are at work all day? How will clients who live alone manage (unassisted) to give oral medications to patients who won't eat it with food? People with certain **disabilities** may not be able to adequately monitor progress or administer treatments.

Remember to always keep in mind the **personal safety** of clients and avoid asking them to do something that puts them at risk of, for example, being bitten, scratched, injured or harmed in some way.

Give An Estimate of Costs

In my opinion, it is **mandatory** to give an estimate (or treatment plan) of proposed treatments and procedures when the cost is greater than the current practice Average Transaction Value (ATV) - normally between £60-75 (at time of writing). Even when clients indicate that they don't need one, give them an estimate anyway; it just **avoids misunderstandings** and wrong assumptions later on.

Please don't purposefully leave it to the receptionist to tell the client, at the front desk, what the cost of treatment has been. Especially if the bill is higher than what the client was expecting, this situation is embarrassing for the client, the receptionist and the people in the reception area. It is a **professional obligation**, in my opinion, for a veterinary surgeon to discuss costs with a client in the privacy of the consulting room.

Remember to give full details of the treatments and tests proposed (i.e. explain the value) ***before*** giving the cost.

Get the Client's Consent. Gain the client's approval before you proceed with care. Explain what the charges will be and get <u>written</u> authorisation and consent to treat the patient. This is a legal requirement to avoid **malpractice**.

Do not omit tests/procedures because of **your perception of what the client can afford!**
Present an estimate for your best recommendations and then **keep quiet** and *let the client decide what is best for them!*
Be careful not to promise a successful outcome. "**Under promise and over deliver**".

Perform Exam Room Procedures & Administer Treatments

Perform Tests and Procedures that you can do *immediately* and within the consulting appointment time e.g.

- Blood tests
- Bandaging
- Wound cleaning
- Skin scrapes
- Fine needle aspirates
- Eye tests: fluorescein, Schirmer tear tests, etc

If this will take longer than the appointment time, then consider *admitting* the patient or performing the tests or treatments at another appointment.

Administer any medications e.g.

- Tablets
- Injections
- Ear/eye drops
- Skin ointment/gel/cream applications

Apart from injections, this also **demonstrates** to clients how to administer any medications dispensed. Again, show them what you are doing. Don't do anything secretively. Make it obvious what you are doing. For example, clients should not be surprised that you have already given the vaccination, or other medication, without them noticing.

Clients will feel more like they have got their money's worth (i.e. received value) if you can justify doing something like giving an injection to start the pet's treatment regimen, administering the first dose of creams, oral medications, etc. Starting off treatments of several days with an injection, also guarantees that the pet has at least received the first dose.

Additionally, giving the pet an injection of a long-acting medication **guarantees** that the pet actually receives the medication instead of asking the client to administer the medication at home, usually multiple times a day. This has the added benefit of **guaranteeing compliance** and providing **ease** and **convenience** for the client - one less task for them to do in their already busy lives.

Give Educational Material

Every client should leave the practice with **tangible evidence** of the service provided!

Try to never let a client leave empty-handed. Give them:

- **Back-up information**: leaflets and handouts pertaining to the problem

- **General advice handouts**: nutrition, dentistry, aging, neutering, behaviour, breed/species information etc.

- An **email** or **text** with a **link** to any relevant information e.g. from www.veterinarypartner.com

Some clients like to educate themselves, so give them the resources and the opportunity to do so. Some want to simply be given *everything* they need.

Make Appointments for Medical Progress Evaluations and In-patient Procedures

Be sure to explain to the client **WHY** you need to see their pet again, and **when**. It helps to give only sufficient medication until the next appointment as it encourages keeping that appointment.

Make **specific** appointments for clients who need to come back. Set a *specific date* and *time* for the procedure/test/progress evaluation/etc and ask the receptionist to make the appointment at the time of the consultation. Leaving the client to remember to make an appointment *drastically* reduces compliance.

Medical Progress Evaluations

Provided the case merits it, arrange to see the patient regularly **until the condition is *completely* resolved**. Please do not leave the decision about whether a pet's condition is completely resolved up to the client. They are not trained to do this no matter how sensible they may appear to be. You are the veterinary surgeon and **only you** should make that decision. Recalls allow us (the trained professionals) to evaluate illnesses and not leave the decisions about when, or if, a pet needs to be seen up to the client. Ask:

*"Mrs Jones, Jake **needs** to be seen again in 2 days, when is a convenient time?"*

Avoid saying, **"Come back in a few days"**. Make an appointment for a specific day and time and, if necessary, put a reminder on the computer for you to remind the client of an upcoming appointment.

Just like you and I, clients often lead remarkably busy lives; we can, and indeed should, give them the help they need with **remembering** and **organising issues related to their pet's health**.

To save time and for simplicity, use the "recall codes" that most practice management systems can generate. These also appear on the invoice and serve as a useful reminder to the receptionist to make the appointment, e.g. our practice used:

- sMon (See again on Monday please)
- s1d (see again tomorrow please)

Remember that Veterinary Medicine is a **continuous activity** for clients and pets and involves an ongoing series of appointments for illnesses and/or preventative healthcare that **does not end** for clients and pets (until the death of the pet)

Try to have an idea of the expected outcome from the previous consultation /evaluation. Ask yourself:

1. What you expect to happen?
2. How will you know if what was expected did not happen or is not happening?
3. What will you do then? **Have a plan!**

Forewarned is Forearmed - Safety Netting

Sometimes, despite our best efforts, things will not go according to plan resulting in **unexpected outcomes**. For example, the antibiotics may not work well, or the patient is still uncomfortable despite taking the analgesics, etc. **Safety-netting** is where you try to prepare the client for all possible outcomes …. just in case the unexpected happens.

Forewarned is forearmed. Make sure to explain to the client what any unexpected outcomes, and possible side effects of some drugs, to look out for, e.g. swelling of the wound, vomiting and diarrhoea, drinking more, urinating more, loss of appetite, etc. You must also explain **what to do about it** e.g.

"If he becomes distressed trying to urinate but can't then he needs to be seen immediately".

"Brandy should feel a lot more comfortable by tomorrow morning, if that's not the case please call us as we may have to try another or additional treatment".

"Many patients tend to drink more and urinate more with this medication. If this becomes unacceptable, please let me know."

Knowing what may happen *before* it happens stands you in good stead with the client, enhancing the trust they have in you and the practice.

Closing the Consultation

Summarise the Agreed-Upon Treatment

This helps clarify what was found, recommended, and decided upon. **Keep it simple**, there is no need to repeat entirely what has previously been discussed. Say something like:

"So, in summary, we are going the treat the cough with antibiotics for 5 days starting tonight, keep Brandy away from other dogs, and see him again on Friday. Is that Ok?"

"OK, we have decided to start the gastro-intestinal prescription tonight, feed 4 meals a day, keep Brandy on a leash on walks so he does not scavenge, and not feed any treats until I see him again on Friday. Is that all alright?"

Close with:

"Have I answered all your questions?"

or

"Have I addressed all your concerns?"

And then address any other questions or concerns that the client may have.

Finally, ask:

"Is There Anything Else That You Would Like To Ask Me?"

This is also a pleasant way to indicate to the client that this is the end of the consultation.

You should not have to worry about opening up a whole new discussion if early on we did a good job of addressing the clients concerns about their pet; it is rare for them to raise any unanswered queries now.

Say, "Goodbye Mr/Mrs/Miss _(owner's name)_. Thank you."

Next say, Goodbye _(pet's name)_ and, if it is a dog, give it a **treat** (if appropriate) and a goodbye **pat/stroke**.

Show the client out to the reception desk (and if appropriate, repeat a reminder of the next visit e.g. "See you next Tuesday").

Send the client home with a **report** (e.g. CPE form) that explains your findings, recommendations, and any instructions.

Keep Optimum Consulting Times

The way to improve consultation outcomes is not necessarily to increase the consultation *time*, but to *improve the way the available time is spent.*

There appears to be an **optimum time** for 1st opinion clients to spend in the exam room. Less than 10-15 mins is probably too short and more that 20-25 mins probably too long.

Trying to adequately address all issues in the allotted consulting time leads to **OVER-RUNNING** and usually also doing a poorer job.

If possible, *sit down* and explain the issues with clients. Studies with human doctors show that clients perceive that they got better care if the doctor **sat down** with them, no matter how briefly.

Have an organised consulting room. This helps by not wasting time trying to find equipment and drugs, etc.

Utilise the nurses (if available). Having a nurse in the consulting room allows for them to perform all the tasks that they are **permitted** and **capable** of doing, so that you only have to do what a veterinarian needs to do: examine, diagnose, explain, treat, and prescribe. *Nurses are invaluable in enhancing the efficiency, effectiveness, productivity and value of the consultation experience.* A nurse with the appropriate training can:

- ✓ Restrain pets competently, which allows for a quicker and more thorough examination (compared of the client restraining their pet)
- ✓ Take blood samples
- ✓ Perform skin scrapes and set up samples for microscopy
- ✓ Talk to the client about parasite control, nutrition, and go through any leaflets given
- ✓ Talk about Health Club membership and pet insurance
- ✓ Book appointments for medical progress evaluations

✓ Keep the exam room clean, tidy, and organised

✓ Etc.

Address the most important 1-2 issues: Tell the client that the others need addressing. Then **schedule follow-up appointments** when these other matters can be more appropriately dealt with. It may be helpful to advise owners that *multiple problems can be approached in a **stepwise** fashion*, dealing with the **most urgent first**.

Sometimes it is more appropriate to say,

"These are the things we need to work on, and *you let me know when, and if, this is something you want to pursue*".

Admit the patient into care, when addressing a problem that is *likely to take longer* than the allotted 15 or 20 mins e.g.

- ○ blood-sampling an uncooperative pet
- ○ wound cleaning
- ○ abscess treatment, etc.

Most owners will consent, especially if you **explain** that the procedure needs more time to do **a more thorough job**.

Say something like:

"Mr Jones, to do a thorough job of cleaning the wound (examining the ear, treating the abscess, etc) it will take more time than we have right now. Do you mind if we admit Rex so that we can spend more time treating him later?"

Remember: Try not to make clients feel that if they don't do anything immediately you will think less of them. Give them a **treatment plan** and *book the follow-up appointments*.

Email or send clients home with a **report** of all the problems identified and what needs to be done about them.

A Team Approach for Addressing Everything

The consultation appointment is typically 15-20 mins long. There is a progressive tendency for longer consultations as clients increasingly expect more value and as in-depth explanations as possible of the medical issues. Many clients seek answers from "Dr Google" before and after a consultation and we find ourselves having to communicate more thoroughly than in the past when it was acceptable to address only the immediate concerns or the urgent, and in a somewhat cursory manner.

With ever-improving nutritional diets, parasite control products, breeding and client knowledge on animal care and welfare, the relatively common and "easy to deal with" medical problems of the past are thankfully becoming rare.

However, we are now moving to a more **proactive** type of medicine where the focus is on prevention and early detection of illnesses.

Reactive medicine is about only responding to the service for which the patient is presented. If we respond only to what clients say they <u>want</u>, we may be ignoring what the pets really *need*.

Proactive care is about *looking for opportunities* to **prevent** problems or diagnose problems early and treat them early. Practising proactive medicine involves more explanation of why it is important to do things like performing senior screening tests, performing stage 1 dentistry, checking for and treating arthritis when symptoms are mild, investigating lumps and bumps when they first appear, encouraging preanaesthetic testing, etc. Doing all this takes the clinician **more time** and **more effort** if done properly.

More skill, and arguably **more knowledge**, is needed when recommending proactive medicine, where the pet seems relatively healthy, than when dealing with obvious and urgent medical problems (reactive medicine). It is quite easy to explain, and get compliance for, the need for dental treatment at stage 3 and 4 disease where symptoms such as halitosis, periodontitis and pain are obvious, than it is to recommend treatment at stage 1 or 2, when clients are not aware of any problems.

During a typical 15-20-minute booster vaccination (wellness) appointment, which may be only time that year that a pet visits the practice, the matters that typically need to be addressed include:

1. A comprehensive 12-body system physical examination
2. Any problems identified proactively such as dental disease, lumps and bumps, overgrown nails, etc
3. Parasite control (fleas, ticks and worms)
4. Nutrition and weight management
5. Practice health club membership
6. Pet insurance

Is it any wonder that vets constantly over-run appointments? With potentially so many areas to address, in so little time, it is hardly surprising that most vets only focus on the **urgent**, and point 2 gets rushed through while points 3, 4, 5 and 6 often get overlooked.

Adopting a **TEAM APPROACH** seems to be the only way to overcome this conundrum. The vet simply cannot, and maybe should not, deal with all the matters in a typical wellness or other consultation. A vet needs to focus on doing only those (high value) things that a vet is licenced to do: examining, diagnosing, administering treatments, prescribing and performing surgery. **Almost everything else can be done by support staff** *once they have been given the right training*. For example, the whole team can help with client education especially on wellness initiatives, and veterinary nurses can also play an active role in history taking, vital signs data capture, body condition scoring, explaining home care instructions, etc.

It takes time and effort to develop a **high-performance team** like this. It requires specific training for the right knowledge, the right skills, and the right behaviours. Every employee must have absolute *CLARITY* on **responsibilities**, **expectations**, and **accountabilities**.

This will remove the "bottle-neck" of the time-poor vet that many practices experience. This approach has worked very well in the practices that I owned and managed. We had nurses assisting the vets in every consultation - they restrained pets for examination and treatment, priced up services, cleaned, tidied, and organised the exam room, etc., which all **saved considerable time** for the vets, allowing them more "**face-time**" with clients to **explain things better**, which invariably lead to higher compliance of recommendations and hence increased revenues which then paid for it all. Vets are also less flustered and less stressed in *trying to do everything*, nurses and receptionists contribute more and feel more valued, and clients get a better and quicker service that they are happier to pay for. Everybody wins!

Part 2: CONSULTING BEHAVIOURS

Introduction

"It is more important to know what sort of person has a disease, than to know what sort of disease a person has" Hippocrates, circa 400BC

Medicine can be described as both a **science** (the *objective* part - scientific evidence, knowledge and technical skills - **what** is done) and an **art** (the *subjective* part - **how** the medicine is delivered and **personalised** to the individual). The science is what is taught at veterinary school and is the major component of most veterinary conferences and continuing education. The art, unfortunately, is still often mostly overlooked and left to developing on the job …. hopefully.

Defining success in veterinary practice can be a difficult and very personal thing. Most often people think it's only all about clinical mastery with regards to medical knowledge and technical skills. However, those attributes do not ensure personal fulfilment, financial and business success. Success in veterinary medicine as a whole therefore, also requires:

- ✓ Communication and interpersonal skills
- ✓ Client service skills
- ✓ Team building and leadership skills
- ✓ Business understanding

In this book, we will only be looking at communication, interpersonal, and client service skills.

Objectives

Every veterinary consultation must include an **understanding** *of the* *CLIENT*.

There is a tendency to focus *only* on the pet and its immediate problem, sometimes totally ignoring the human who brought the pet in and who will need to make health-care decisions based on **THEIR understanding** of what is going on.

A vet **MUST** be able to properly and effectively *COMMUNICATE* and ensure a **client's understanding** of:

- ✓ examination findings
- ✓ a diagnosis
- ✓ treatment options and plans
- ✓ a prognosis
- ✓ the costs involved

IT CAN BE ARGUED THAT A VET WHO IS UNABLE TO DO THIS HAS FAILED AT THEIR JOB!

The Client-Vet Relationship

Veterinary medicine today involves an almost equal *integration* of **technical medical** skills and **client service** skills.

Clients are the gateway to helping pets and the *quality* of our **relationships** with clients depends on the *quality* of our **communications** with them! It is important to communicate *clearly*, *effectively* and *sensitively*.

Veterinary medicine's biggest challenge today is communicating EXACTLY *what* we do for pets, and *why.*

Owners don't get it because we don't *explain* it!

Inadequate communication between veterinary surgeons and clients is **THE** leading cause of client dissatisfaction (and perhaps also the reason that clients don't always follow our recommendations).

We are, actually, all **teachers** because our clients are paying us imparting our *knowledge*, the things that we know, to them They did not attend veterinary school, so it is in essence our obligation to communicate our knowledge to them. Every client interaction is an opportunity to **teach** about **pet care**. In fact, we have the opportunity to teach thousands of people in our practices, and we are responsible for the health and wellbeing of all our patients.

"As veterinary doctors, one of our highest ideals should be guiding clients to understanding of illnesses (and death)" Adapted: Paul Kalanithi

If a pet dies from a disease for which we had a preventative or a treatment that we never told the client about, that pet's death is arguably our fault.

It is *our* job to **educate** the client about what products, actions or services would benefit their pet.

It is *their* job to **decide** which ones they want.

The only way you can take good care of patients is to **educate their owners** on how to take care of their pets and which healthcare decisions, including medical treatments, to choose.

Also, veterinary team members with good communication skills are more likely to have greater job satisfaction and less work-related stress.

How to Build Trust and Rapport

Trust needs to be **earned**, it is not freely given, and one of our primary objectives is to **build trusting relationships** with clients. Remember that having the best medical skills (clinical and surgical) is useless unless clients have **trust** and **allow you** to use those skills on their pets.

It seems that we as human beings are wired to make **instant judgements** of others – confident or unsure, good looking or not, exciting or boring, personable or not, friendly or unfriendly, etc. How we make these judgements appears to be based on often quite whimsical **observations** – our appearance and the way we dress, how we stand, walk or sit, our facial expressions and body language, how we speak, etc.

In light of this, the **first few minutes** of the initial pet owner-vet relationship is particularly important for creating trust and rapport. It has been shown that establishing trust and rapport is an important contributor to improved medical care, easing client anxiety, and increasing pet-owners' involvement in the decisions about their pet's care.

Appearance

What would your ideal client expect you to look like?
Dress like a **professional**. Be **smart** and **well-presented**.
We must always be conscious of our personal appearance. Clients often make a judgement of our practice and the medical care we provide by the way we **dress,** the way we **present ourselves**.

Having Confidence and Providing Reassurance

Demonstrate confidence by genuinely **believing** in what you are saying (the advice you are giving). If you are confident about what you are saying, the client will perceive this and have confidence in you and the care you provide.

Have positive energy and enthusiasm. Have an expectation of a positive outcome. This will help clients to trust you.

Reassure clients by:
- Explaining medical concepts in simple terms - don't use medical jargon
- Letting clients know that you will do everything you can to help their pet; that you have **their best interests** at heart
- Not being judgemental about the way they have cared for their pet and the decisions they make
- Involving them in the medical decision-making process e.g. "What do you think about this treatment plan?
  How does that sound?
  Does this work for you?
  Is that feasible for you?
  Are you comfortable with that?"
- Etc.

Being Reliable

This is one of the **highest-rated positive traits that clients look for** in a service industry like ours.
Do **what** you said you would, do it **when** you said you would, and do it **how** you said you would.

Let clients know, *in advance*, when you are *unable* to do _exactly_ what you said you would or when and/or how you said you would.

We are **advocates** for the health needs of our patients and our clients depend on us for a service that is competent and reliable.

Clients come to us because we offer them **PEACE OF MIND** (and hope) that we can solve their pet-related concerns and because they trust us to offer them the best recommendations at the best value.

Listening Carefully (Active Listening)

Look interested. Keep your focus on the client, not on the computer screen. Listen to **understand**, not just to respond. Listen for the client's point of view. Try to get some idea of what the pet means to them.

Paraphrase to ensure you understand what they say by repeating back using different words e.g.

"So, you're worried about the pimples and red patch under her chin?"

Let the client speak without interrupting - they will then be more likely to listen to what **you** have to say and be more willing to accept your recommendations. Clients need to feel that they have had an opportunity to voice **all** their concerns.

It is especially important not to interrupt at the **start** of the consultation to ensure that the first concern is **not** the most important or **only** concern.

You might even have an idea of what the problem is before the client finishes explaining. Resist the temptation to "butt-in" even if you think that it will save time. Trying to hurry the consultation by interrupting often does not save any more time and usually results in drawing the wrong conclusions, making poorer medical decisions, and in reduced client satisfaction. Surveys with medical doctors indicate that, on average, a doctor interrupts a patient within 18 seconds!

Expressing Empathy

Be **warm** and **empathetic**. When we show empathy towards others, they are more likely to be more open and receptive to what we have to say.

Empathy is: **Compassionate Understanding** of how the other person might be feeling; the ability to identify with and understand somebody else's feelings or difficulties.

Examples of phrases that demonstrate empathy include:

"I understand......."
"I see why......."
"I can see how worried/sad/frustrated you are"
"Clearly this seems to be worrying you a lot"
"If I understand you properly .... "
"Under the same circumstances, I'm sure that I would feel the same"

Do not minimise a client's frustration or concern. What may be something minor *to you*, may be a source of real distress *for them*. Our experience, competence and knowledge as veterinary professionals can lead us to have a type of bias where, because we have seen or dealt with much worse problems before, we tend to trivialise less serious problems.

Ways to show empathy:
- ✓ **Touch** - *when appropriate*, lightly on top of hand or shoulder
- ✓ **Pause** - allows time to reflect on what has been said
- ✓ **Ask** questions - How can I help?
- ✓ **Listen** - Be an "active listener"

Limit any fidgets such as fidgeting with hair, tapping fingers, covering mouth, etc.
If nervous, try gently stroking the pet.

And remember, it's not just the words you use that convey empathy, how you say them, a genuine smile and active listening play an important part.

Professional Standards

Personal Hygiene
Personal cleanliness is very important. Body and oral malodour are not appropriate.
Keep hair clean, well-groomed and in an appropriate style. Men with beards and moustaches must keep them neatly trimmed. Fingernails should be clean and trimmed. Bright nail polish or excessively long fingernails are not appropriate. Excessive make-up, perfume, cologne, aftershave or heavy jewellery is not appropriate. These seemingly small details can have a powerful impact.

Dress
Clients often make a judgement of you and your practice by the way you dress. DRESS LIKE A PROFESSIONAL; it is an easy way to get respect and attention. Looking and feeling professional will also give you added personal confidence which will come across to the client.

The practice uniform must be worn when on duty in the practice or acting on behalf of the practice elsewhere. The uniform must be clean and freshly pressed. Always be conscious of your personal appearance.

Timekeeping
An appointment is a **social contract**, so **BE ON TIME**.

If you are running late, say "Thank you for waiting" and leave it at that. This is better than saying "I'm sorry about the wait", which has a negative connotation to it.

If clients are obviously upset about waiting, then acknowledge their annoyance and frustration by saying "I understand that it can be frustrating to be kept waiting".

Try to explain that you were doing something **_specific_** (e.g. blood sampling, comforting a distressed client, cleaning a large wound, etc.), rather than just say that you were "busy"

Common Courtesy
Be mindful of common courtesies:
- ✓ Say "please", "thank you" and "goodbye"
- ✓ Open doors for clients
- ✓ Help carry bags of food, packets, pets, etc.
- ✓ Shake Hands

The formal, accepted touch is the handshake. We encourage shaking hands with clients _when it is convenient to do so._

People have sensitivity to touch from others so we must learn how to use touch effectively. The handshake, for example, must be **firm** but **not strong**, **brief** but neither too short nor too long a grip. Needless to say, hands must be clean.

Personal Space
Respect a reasonable distance between you and the person you are speaking with. Although some people may have a very short distance between them and another person the average person needs at least two to three feet to feel comfortable. Keep your distance in mind!

Maintain Full Body Posture

- Our body reflects our energy level. If we are slouched people might think that we are tired or bored. If we are actively doing something else while speaking to someone they infer that we are too busy for them. So we must always be aware of the need to focus on the person we are speaking with and not look at our watch, tidy up, continue to type at a keyboard etc

- Maintain your face and body towards the client.

- Maintain a **slight forward lean** - try to stand on the balls of your feet. By leaning slightly forward we give the person we are speaking with the sense that we are engaged with them and interested in what they are saying.

Hands and Arms

- The way we hold our hands and move them communicates feelings as well. If we clench our fists, we send the message of anger or impatience whereas if we open our hands, we are being more open and honest. If we move our hands too much, we can distract the person from listening to our words. If we have absolutely no hand movements we are seen as uninterested, perhaps even uninteresting to the listener.
- Learn to use open-handed gestures but be aware of your hands to ensure that you are not trying to "speak with your hands".
- Don't fold your arms (gives the impression that you are not receptive)

Facial Expression

Our face is a mirror to our emotions. Everyone around us can see whether we are having a good day or a bad day – even whether we had a tiresome night!

Be conscious of your facial expression. No-one needs to know that you are having a bad day or are in a bad mood.

Concentrate on having a *calm and friendly expression* even when there is chaos around you (equanimity). It helps to be mindful of your own state of mind, your personal feelings and emotions, and practice not making negative feelings obvious to those around you.

Rapport means **friendly relationship**. The Cambridge English dictionary defines rapport as: a good understanding of someone and an ability to communicate well with them.

It is an emotional bond or friendly relationship between people based on mutual liking, trust, and a sense that they understand and share each other's concerns.

Establishing rapport is facilitated by being **relaxed** and as **genuine**, **authentic** and **true** to your _personality_ as possible. It is easily destroyed by trying to be the person you think your client wants you to be.

In Summary

- ✓ Be friendly
- ✓ Be interested
- ✓ Talk about the client's special interest
- ✓ Use the client's name
- ✓ Smile
- ✓ Be open and honest

First Impressions

"Everyone sees what you appear to be, few experience what you really are" (Machiavelli)

First impressions really do matter. Studies show that within 10-30 seconds of meeting someone an individual has developed an impression of that person's competence, confidence and enthusiasm (Dr Nalini Ambady, Harvard professor of social psychology). Be warm and welcoming.

The previous appointment may have been a difficult case with an extremely sick pet, or even a euthanasia, and now your next appointment is an excited client with a new puppy. As difficult as it may be, try to ignore the previous interaction and its associated emotions and focus all of your attention the next task at hand, on the patient and client in front of you. This **is not easy**, and it takes practice to **collect your thoughts**, **prepare yourself mentally**, **fully focus on the current task** and **present your best self** to the next client.

It is one of the **challenges of veterinary medicine** – having so many things to do and think about, *all at the same time*, but needing to **put it all to one side** and focus entirely on the client and patient in front of you. This is a **skill** that you need to develop and keep practicing.

Greeting

Confidently enter the consulting room, make eye contact, smile and greet the client. Entering the consulting room with **positive energy** and a calm and friendly disposition will reduce anxiety and alleviate the annoyance of waiting clients.

Offer an enthusiastic "hello" and a sincere smile to every client, *unless* you anticipate breaking bad news or dealing with particularly distressed and anxious clients.

Greet **clients** and their **pets** by name. Greet their **children**.

Although you may have seen and greeted many clients that day, it is the first time that you are greeting *that* particular client.

It is up to you to show clients that they have made the right choice in coming to your practice, and that your team is **caring, friendly** and **enthusiastic**.

Smile

Remember the power of smiling. Yes, I know you've heard this before; but IT DOES WORK!

A natural, genuine smile creates trust. Smiling alters your tone of voice, making you sound more positive and interested. Smiling immediately transforms you physically so that you will come across as **warm** and **friendly** – even though there may be stressful situations in the practice. Your smile needs to be genuine as people can easily distinguish a genuine from a fake smile; and a fake smile leads to mistrust, the opposite of what you're after.

A smile and enthusiasm are contagious. Also true for a <u>bad</u> attitude. Clients and employees like to be in happy and positive places.

Make Eye Contact

One of the most important things we can do to achieve more effective communication is through making **eye contact**. It shows the client that they have your full and undivided attention. Lack of eye contact can often imply **disinterest** and **indifference**.

Make eye contact as you speak to the client (3-5 seconds is ideal as a rule of thumb). Excessive eye contact makes people uncomfortable so **don't stare**.

We must learn to make immediate eye contact with anyone with whom we are going to speak; maintain eye contact during the conversation but look away from time to time to ensure that we are not making the person uncomfortable.

Eye contact actually improves communication through making us focus on what the person is saying because we are *seeing* them speak and paying attention to them.

When people are emotional there is a tendency to look away. In veterinary practice, much of what we do has a strong emotional element to it. To show that we care we must develop the skill of maintaining eye contact *during emotional discussions* to show that we care.

Compliment The Pet and Client

Although we are generally trained to look for medical **problems**, in other words what is *wrong*, make an effort to notice, and praise, the owner and pet for what is being done right.

Everyone's ego needs, and enjoys, occasional stroking.

During a physical examination **verbalise** the **good** findings e.g.
- "Casey has wonderful teeth"
- "Well done for managing to keep her ideal weight so well controlled"
- "Isn't he well-behaved"
- "What a nice shiny coat you (the pet) have!"
- "You're doing a great job keeping Brutus in excellent health"

Every pet has something positive about which you can compliment: cute, pretty, clean, well-behaved, gorgeous, sleek, fuzzy, clever, healthy, adventurous, sweet etc.

Clients like to hear complimentary things about themselves and their loved ones. Parents can tell you that when people say nice things about their children, it's equivalent to saying nice things about _them_. It has the same impact when hearing nice things about their pets. You can always find something nice to say, however, praise does need to be **genuine** and **true**, and said in a meaningful manner.

Tell clients what a good job they are doing if they are. If they could be doing a better job, then be helpful and **sympathetic** in letting them know how to do better.

Reinforce their actions by saying, "You did the right thing by bringing Smokey in today." Nobody likes to feel that they wasted their time, your time, and also paid for the privilege! It may have been only a minor medical problem or an unnecessary worry to you but giving peace of mind to pet owners is **invaluable** to them and much appreciated.

Praise clients when they have done something that you know may have been difficult for them e.g. keeping a pet indoors, having a pet wear an Elizabethan collar 24/7, getting a urine sample, etc. Clients can be proud that they had to do something that was

hard for them or expensive for them, but it has been *worth it* because the pet is better. This will help to **encourage** the client to take pride in their compliance efforts and in their pet's improvement.

Give Treats

Give every pet a treat - a really tasty one! As long as it is medically appropriate to do so – e.g. not for gastro-intestinal cases.

The treat needs to be a super-tasty one so that the pet is "distracted" from the stress of the veterinary visit and all that is being done to it there. With repeat visits, hopefully the pet then starts to associate the veterinary visit with a **pleasant experience**. It converts an otherwise "ALL STRESS" experience into an "ALL TREAT" one.

Interact with the Pet

Clients like to see contact or interaction with their pets and a fuss being made of them.

Lavish the pet with *genuine* positive praise. Praising and petting pets (whilst also giving them a treat as mentioned above) will go a long way to alleviating the fear and anguish of the veterinary visit for both the pet and the owner.

Clients want to *feel* that you **LIKE** them and their pets.

Pet/stroke the animal and talk to it as you discuss its medical problems and symptoms with the owner.

If the pet's condition is profoundly serious, and the time appears appropriate, **lightly touch** the top of the client's hand or shoulder when you tell them the news.

It is **up to you** to instil confidence in the pet and the owner.

Making Clients Feel Like Number One

Try to make every client contact an exceptional experience by making every client **feel** especially important.

"They may forget your name, but they will never forget how you made them feel." Maya Angelou

To be a successful vet you need to learn to match the **science** with the **soul**!

Service is judged by the quality and strength of the *emotional connection* that you make with the client. It's all about *feelings*.

People may hear your words, but they <u>FEEL</u> your *ATTITUDE*!

The best professionals, in any of the professions, are those who care about their clients/customers as fellow human beings - and show them that they **genuinely do care**!

Basic Service on its own is important but is not enough – it is what is *expected*, and by itself doesn't make anyone *feel* special.
Making the **Emotional Connection** is what is what is needed to make clients *feel* like number one!

Modern Clients

Increasingly, clients are developing a deep emotional attachment to their pets. Pets are part of the family and provoke all the sentiments and feelings associated with that relationship.

So, as I'm sure you have heard before, clients really don't care how much you know until they know how much you care!

And, although you may care more than anyone else in the world, unless you COMMUNICATE that care, and *DEMOSTRATE* that care, in a way that they can *easily* <u>see</u> or <u>understand</u>, they will think that you are **indifferent**. This indifference is one of the main reasons that clients lose trust and leave one practice for another.

When clients come in for a consultation, they are often frightened or worried, nervous, intimidated or don't understand.

By putting yourself in your clients' shoes (i.e. being empathetic) you can make their experience (and yours) much more pleasant and easier, and this builds trust and rapport.

Remember that **new clients** are at first a "trial user" - testing the waters, so to speak. They are deciding if your practice is a good match for them and their pet.

It is worth noting that they will often judge the quality of your services (how good you are) by how you *treat* **THEM**, how you make them *feel*, not by the actual medical care given to their pet!

Take Personal Interest

Unless it is an anticipated emergency or a serious medical problem, take the first few moments of a consultation to ask about the client personally. Don't delve straight into the medicine. Ask about:

- How the pet got its name
- The pet's favourite toy, treat, etc.
- Clients hobbies/interests
- Children's names: how they are finding school, what their interests are
- The weather
- Sporting events
- Etc.

Churn their *emotions* before you churn their *intellect*!

Kindle the *heart* before you kindle the *head!*

Find common interests with clients. e.g. a shared favourite breed, sport, hobby, books, etc. If the client has the same mobile phone as you ask them how they find it. Makes notes about first names, interests, etc. in the client record to help you remember for next time.

All people want to be liked and studies show that doctors are perceived by their clients as more caring and competent when the doctors *seem to like them*.

Also, if clients seem to like *you*, you will enjoy your job much more, your stress levels will be reduced, and the likelihood of complaints against you will fall.

Take the Time

Always take the time to make clients feel special

Taking the time to engage in **friendly talk** (casual exam room conversation) with a client shows clients that:

1) you have time for them
2) that they are not just part of an assembly line and
3) that your doctor-client relationship is important

This helps to create a feeling in clients of being understood by their veterinarian and so increases their levels of trust. However, *too much friendly talk* will detract from the examination time and one must remember to shift quickly away to the task at hand.

Don't appear hurried, even if you are! No one wants a doctor who seems to be in a hurry. Learn to cultivate a relaxed presence. Develop **equanimity**, which is calmness and composure especially in a difficult situation.

If you have kept a client waiting, say,

"Thank you for your patience"

... rather than "Sorry for keeping you for waiting", the latter apology has negative connotations and reinforces a bad experience.

Although we should strive not to keep clients waiting, remember that often people don't mind having to wait for excellent service, but it needs to be excellent.

Use Names – Call Every Client and Pet by Name

Calling every client and pet by name is more powerful than you might think. It is courteous and an easy way to get and keep the person's attention. If you remember a client's name it will make them **feel important**, respected and help develop a positive relationship with you and the practice. It's like "you know them" personally.

For difficult to pronounce names <u>**do not**</u> hazard a guess as this can offend some people. Simply ask,

"Can I please ask you how to pronounce your name"

As someone with a somewhat difficult to pronounce surname, I can tell you that I really appreciate being asked how to pronounce it, rather than correct them.

Please **commit** to remembering clients' names. With committed practice one can fairly easily remember the names of both clients and pets. Check the appointment and patient record to make sure you know the names. Use notes in the clinical record to help with hard to remember pronunciation and the names of children and significant others. For clients and pets that are visiting the practice e.g. to collect something, and you incidentally see them in the reception area, "secretly" ask a colleague who they are before talking to them.

"Not being good with names" is often a poor excuse.

Practice High-Touch, High-Tech Medicine

Involve the client where possible e.g.
- Listening to the heart
- Feeling the crepitus in arthritic joints
- Seeing the parasites, especially under the microscope
- Seeing the discharge in ears, the gingivitis in mouths
- Smelling halitosis

Use and demonstrate the technology that you have available to use in the practice:
- microscope
- video otoscope
- stethoscope - let them listen to the heart murmur
- digital x-rays and dental x-rays
- Ultrasound images
- Laser
- Blood pressure machine
- Photos of conditions or objects found like foreign bodies

Take photos of wounds, bad teeth, etc, that you can email to clients.

Going The Extra Mile

Little acts of kindness! Surprise clients with your **thoughtfulness** and diligence e.g.

- ✓ **Taking the time** to clearly explain exam findings, lab results, treatments, etc. and ensure the client understands what you have explained
- ✓ **Getting advice** from specialists when researching a difficult case
- ✓ Calling clients after work to discuss test results or patient progress
- ✓ **Unexpected care** telephone calls to find out how patients are doing (leaving a message or sending a text message has the same desirable impact)
- ✓ being **respectful of their time** (not keeping them waiting!)
- ✓ Giving **undivided attention** and listening actively (with interest) to their concerns

These **small acts of kindnesses** are examples of "Going the Extra Mile".

Let clients know that you have done extra research, spoken to specialists or colleagues, etc. to try to help their pet.

It is very endearing to clients to realise that you have been thinking about their pets **just because you care**: how they are progressing, making sure they are more comfortable, researching to solve difficult problems, etc.

Human beings seem to be unconsciously wired for the need to reciprocate. If I do something nice for you, then (all things being equal) you'll want to do something nice for me. This is one of the reasons that you receive sentiments of gratitude in the form of thank you cards, chocolates, wine, etc. But do nice things, go the extra mile in other words, because *it's the right thing to do*, not because you simply want to get thanks and appreciation.

In Summary
To make clients feel really special, like they are truly number one,

Take Care of their FEELINGS

If you do this well you won't have to worry much about building trust and rapport and getting compliance with the best healthcare recommendations.

How to Make a Recommendation

As veterinary surgeons, it is our responsibility to look after the welfare of pets entrusted to our care. To do this effectively involves not only accurately diagnosing health problems but **educating** pet owners and *getting their consent* to perform the tests and treatments that are necessary.

Knowing **how** to make recommendations helps to obtain higher **compliance** (adherence) of needed care. Strategies that increase compliance will increase both the welfare of animals under your care and practice success.

Vets are good at identifying the needs that pets have, i.e. making a diagnosis, but relatively **poor** at making a good recommendation and especially at *following through* to ensure the recommendation has actually been carried out.

Most veterinary staff have a primary desire to help animals, from receptionists to vets. Despite this, most practices are woefully deficient at making effective recommendations, as is evidenced by poor compliance rates e.g. for dentistry, senior care, parasite preventatives, etc. Why is this so? Possible reasons include:

1. Lack of knowledge and hence a lack of confidence
2. Poor communication techniques
3. Fear of rejection

Below are useful tips to overcome these obstacles and to make an effective recommendation:

1. Be **knowledgeable** about the service or product that you are recommending. You must know it well in order to talk confidently about it and especially to advise on it. Overcoming nerves and

speaking confidently is something everyone can develop with practice.

2. **Avoid using the word "recommend"** especially when talking about services. Use the word "**need**" instead. In other words, "Mrs Jones, Pip *needs* to have a dental scale and polish" instead of "Mrs Jones, I *recommend* that Pip has a dental scale and polish". "Pip needs to start weight reduction diet" instead of "I recommend that Pip starts a weight control diet". The word "recommend" could imply that something is simply advised but not essential.

3. Talk in terms of the **benefits** of the service or product to the pet and owner. What problem/frustration will the service or product solve?

    "Mrs Jones, after Pip has had his dental treatment, he will **feel** better, his breath **won't smell**, any **pain** he may be experiencing will be eliminated, he might **start eating** that dry diet you've been trying to get him to eat".

    Make **benefits** to the pet obvious. E.g. fresh breath, quicker-healing, less inappropriate urination, etc. This will be the reason for the "pain" of inconvenience, hard work, costs, etc. They need something to look forward to.

4. **Always look for a win-win situation.** It is important for the client to believe that you share the *same ultimate goal* as them:

    - ✓ a healthy pet
    - ✓ pain-free
    - ✓ as comfortable as possible
    - ✓ as happy as possible, etc.

5. **Avoid using terms that are too technical**, to ensure understanding. Most people will not tell you when they are confused to avoid seeming silly. Paraphrase to ensure understanding. **Check**

understanding frequently to make sure clients really understand what you are explaining

6. **Stand beside the client** when discussing needed services, products, and their prices. This helps to foster rapport (i.e. building client relations). Standing directly opposite another person has implications of confrontation instead of connection. Try to face the other person at least by about a **30 to 45-degree angle** especially whilst sitting.

7. Try to give explanations in **easily manageable amounts** – i.e. do not overwhelm clients with too much information all at once. It can be too much to think about and digest.

8. **Make it easy** (simple). E.g. where possible, once daily dosing as opposed to twice daily. Schedule telephone follow-ups to remind clients about care instructions e.g. wound cleansing, ear cleaning, etc
Ask: "Does this seem like something you could do?"

9. Try to **give information** in a **more than one way**: verbal, drawing, handout, link to website, etc.

10. Remember **matching** and **mirroring** techniques with respect to body posture, mannerisms, tone of voice, loudness of voice, and the words you use. You need to try to match these to the clients you are talking to. This again helps to foster better rapport.

11. **Don't become disheartened** or dejected when someone does not take up what you have suggested – they may be declining for reasons beyond your control. Do not **assume** that clients decline your recommendations mostly because of the cost. Studies suggest this is usually not the case; it's more about failing to understand the value or the benefit.

12. **Don't be pushy**. Make your recommendation, then **keep quiet** and allow the client to respond. Avoid making clients feel guilty.

13. Your job is to **educate** clients on what is needed and the options available – only the client can **choose** the best option for themselves. Discuss treatment and investigation choices openly with clients so that they **feel part of the decision-making process** and so take ownership or accountability. This helps in persuading clients and getting compliance with your recommendations. Ask:

    "How does that sound? Does this work for you? Is that feasible for you? Are you comfortable with that?"

14. **Timing** is important. Know **when** and **how much** to discuss. Identify the problem <u>during</u> the examination, **but wait until the explanation phase <u>afterwards</u>** to discuss the recommended treatment e.g. excess weight, dental disease, painful joints, etc.

15. **Convey Value**. Before convincing anyone else of the value of something **YOU** first have to be convinced on its value. Try to get to know *what* the client values e.g. convenience, time, cost, simple treatments, convenience vs effectiveness, control vs cure, etc.

    Sometimes clients will share your values about the importance of certain aspects of their pet's health care, other times they will not. Clients don't really choose one practice over another only on the basis of prices, but rather on the basis of **higher perceived value** that is *demonstrably* offered. **Value** is a combination of <u>price</u> and *perceived* <u>quality</u> and <u>benefits</u>.

16. If clients ask you what you would do, **be honest** – it may help to think what you would do if the patient belonged to a close relative of your significant other.

In summary

1. Ensure you have more than sufficient **knowledge** and training in the areas where compliance is desired, e.g. dentistry and senior care
2. **Practice** making a recommendation: Role plays, video recordings, see how successful people do it.
3. Genuinely **believe** in the recommendation – that it actually is in the interests of the pet and owner.
4. Know when, and in how much detail, to discuss recommendations. If a client seems obviously disinterested, then maybe giving a leaflet is best. "Mr Smith, here's a leaflet for more information on dental disease"
5. Learn to deal with **rejection**.

Assume most objections are based on a lack of knowledge and understanding and <u>not</u> price, and this underpins the need to educate, to teach.

The Fear of Making A Recommendation

When pets have **complicated** and/or **many** problems that need investigating or treating, it can be daunting to recommend **everything** that is necessary and then also present an estimate of how much it all **costs**. For example, when you see a dog for a vaccination, and it has allergies, bad ears, bad teeth and arthritis you would be denying patients' optimum veterinary care if you shy away from making the necessary recommendations.

Tell owners what their pet *needs* and what you need to do to accomplish that, and then **keep quiet** and *let them decide*. Most clients, who initially refrain, often end up getting the needed care over time.

We need to get past the **discomfort** of delivering difficult news, talking about hard to manage conditions, and also their associated costs, with clients. No-one has the right to deny a particular product or service that could truly help. Clients have the right to say no, but *you don't have the right to say it for them!*

Nobody likes presenting clients with a long list of problems and a huge estimate to resolve them all. Nevertheless, if you don't do this then the pet gets "short-changed" and, really, so does the client, and the practice. They would have brought the pet to us because they care about its well-being (already doing more than many pet owners). They are willing to pay a consultation fee to get your opinion and recommendation based on you having the knowledge and expertise that they don't have and cannot find elsewhere. Remind yourself about this and it will be easier to deal with. Sometimes you have to "throw everything at them" but *is that not your job?* Doing any less would be doing the patient and yourself an injustice.

Avoid practising band-aid medicine. **Recommend** and **use** the *diagnostic skills* that you learned at vet school. Give the client all the available **options**, then discuss the **best** options and the costs, and then *LET THEM* make a choice.

The Money Talk

Talking about **money** and talking about **euthanasia** are arguably, for most team members, the two most difficult things to talk about in veterinary healthcare. Unfortunately, these are not things that can be avoided in private practice.

We must remember that veterinary healthcare is predominantly a service-based business, where fees are charged for services performed. Furthermore, private practice still depends on clients' **discretionary** spending; apart from some charities, there is no support for personal pet medical care e.g. from the government.

Financial considerations for medical care seem to be directly at odds with the idea that we are a **caring** and **compassionate** profession. Knowing this, and that clients themselves need to fund medical care, which can often cost hundreds and increasingly thousands of pounds, is perhaps one of the main reasons we prefer to avoid talking about money. Also, clients can sometimes make you feel guilty about fees, saying things like:
"I just cannot afford that, I will have to consider euthanasia",
"How much? How do you justify such high fees?",
"All you seem to care about is the money", etc.

It is hardly surprising to try to dodge the money talk if a client has said

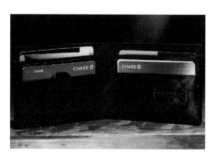

things like this. As the saying goes "once bitten, twice shy." However, it is worth keeping in mind that you cannot continue to provide excellent medical care and wonderful customer service if you do not get paid.

To feel comfortable talking about fees to clients you have to be comfortable with the **value** of the **level of care** that you provide. For pet owners to appreciate the value of the care that you provide you need to **educate** them about the **value of care** that they receive. Until we do that well, the value of veterinary healthcare will always be questioned and diminished.

Focus your client education on **what** needs to be done and **_why_** it needs to be done *before* you talk about how much it all **costs**.

A consultation by definition is a sharing/imparting of knowledge /ideas. Provided you are doing this well, it has value, even if you have not given any tangible treatment, and should have an appropriate fee attached to it which clients should be content pay for.

It is **up to us** to find a way to convert our knowledge and skills into something that a pet owner **understands** and is **willing to pay for** (i.e. something worth exchanging their hard-earned money for).

Clients will always be content to pay for a service that **they** perceive has value.

What to Say and How to Say It

After explaining _what_ needs to be done and _why_, **look the clients in the eye and say**:

"That will be £xxxx.xx (e.g. £1675.00)"

Be **NICE** and **ASSERTIVE**, and CASUAL (as if you do this every day), then **KEEP QUIET** and let them decide. "Speak only if it improves upon the silence" Mahatma Gandhi

Practice just saying it e.g. "That will be £538.00".

Practice using high numbers! Whatever the cost/price is, ***practice just saying it out loud*** and become comfortable with just saying it as if this was completely normal for you...... and before you know it, it _will_ be normal for you.

Don't apologise for the cost of treatments, or make a little joke about it, in an effort to soften the blow e.g. "Hope you're sitting down .... " or "I'm so sorry, it's a large bill, you may want to sit down .... "

If they cringe at the cost, then they cringe. You did your job (and expectation) to the best of your ability – *the decision to refrain from needed care is **theirs***.

If we have done a good job of giving **estimates**, and **keeping clients informed** of on-going costs, then the bill will not be a surprise to them.

How to Deal With Multiple Patient Problems

Trying to adequately address ALL issues in the _limited_ consulting time leads to over-running and usually also doing a poorer job.

Some clients may wait for the annual health and vaccination appointment to present **all** the pet's problems – sometimes in an effort to avoid a separate consultation fees.   They may be expecting you to uncover all these problems and will likely be disappointed if you don't.

Address the **most important 1-2 issues**; _tell the client that the others_ _need addressing_. Then schedule follow-up appointments when these other matters can be more appropriately dealt with. If possible, <u>sit down</u> and explain the issues with clients. Studies with GPs show clients perceive that they got better care if the doctor **sat down**, no matter how briefly.

It may be helpful to advise owners that multiple problems can be approached in a **stepwise** fashion, dealing with the most urgent first. Sometimes it is more appropriate to say,

"These are the things we need to work on, and you let me know when _and if this is something you want to pursue"._

Try not to make clients feel that if they don't do anything immediately you will think less of them. Give them a **treatment plan** and book the **follow-up appointments**.

Send clients home with a **report** of all the problems identified and what needs to be done about them.

What To Do When You Don't Know

Just be honest

*Consulting becomes much more enjoyable when you start appreciating that you **don't need to know everything**, you are **not expected to**, and you don't have to **pretend** that you do.*

Clients really don't mind if you don't know. If you can look the client in the eye and say: **THE TRUTH**

"Look, I'm not sure what's going on here, but I'm going to find out",

... then clients are often satisfied and/or very forgiving of that.

It takes some courage to admit that you do not know something when **you** think that others expect that you should. Medical knowledge is increasing at a dramatic rate and people **do not expect you to know everything** straight away.

Clients just **need to believe** that you are **trying your best** to resolve the problem.

If you just stand there and mumble something, perhaps sprinkled with some complicated medical terms, then that *does not* instil any confidence in the client.

You need to be able to comfortably speak to people, not simply RECITE TECHNICAL TERMS, to ensure the client can understand what you are trying to explain and what their choices are. For example, you can say:

"In my opinion, there is a good chance that these symptoms are caused by one of these 3 conditions; this is what we need to do to narrow the list down ...."

*"In the modern era with so much medical knowledge and information, the pinnacle of being a great vet is not about <u>knowing</u> all the answers, it's about knowing **how** and **where** to <u>find</u> the answers."*

So, it's OK not to know.

It's in **looking things up** and then <u>***you***</u> **finding the answers** that the **magic** is found.

End On A Positive Note

ALWAYS try to make the visit end on a POSITIVE note.

Tell the client:

 "You made the right decision bringing Bruno in today, he's lucky to have such a caring/observant owner"

Wrap Up/Goodbye

We started with a greeting, so we should end with:

1. A smile
2. Offering reassurance

   "If you have concerns please call at any time"

3. Bidding a sincere "Goodbye"

Don't Forget To Follow Up

Follow-ups (or progress evaluations) are the **key** to health and well-being for our patients. They give **peace of mind to pet owners** and help us **build trusting relationships** with clients.

Telephone Follow-Ups (TFUs)

Clients should receive telephone follow-up's until they, and the vet, are satisfied that the problem has been resolved.

Although it is preferable for the vet who saw the client (and patient) to call, if they can't, then please ensure a nurse or receptionist makes the call; but they must refer to the attending vet during the conversation:

"Hello, this is Meena, one of the nurses at Vet Practice. Dr. Paul asked me to call you just to check in and find out how Toffee is doing today."

The client will probably remember the vet from the visit.

You can add a **personal touch** and improve **at-home education** by using SMS and e-mail as well. It is often "the thought that counts", so leaving a telephone message or sending a text or email is often as impactful as a personal conversation.

Sincere follow-up calls not only help endear us to clients, but also can help us better understand both patient and client needs.

Remember, It's All About Building Relationships

In this age of the "modern client," plus constant medical and technological advancements, we need to continuously work to develop and refine the **relationship** between the **veterinary team** and **pet owners**.

For practice, team and individual success it is *building* relationships that has taken centre stage!

Printed in Great Britain
by Amazon